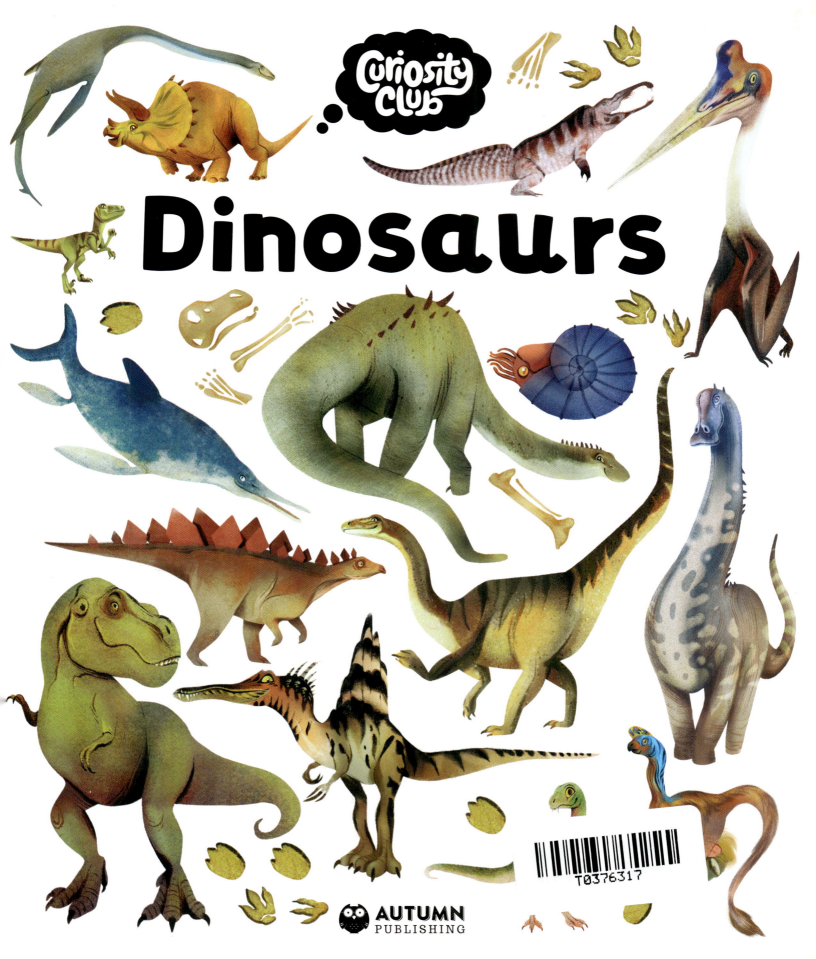

# Good to Know!

You'll come across some very useful words in this book!
Here's what they all mean...

**Amphibian:** an animal that can live both in water and on land.

**Apex Predator:** a dinosaur or animal at the top of the food chain without any predators of its own.

**Arthropod:** a type of invertebrate with an exoskeleton and a segmented body.

**Carnivore:** a dinosaur or animal that only eats meat.

**Climate:** the weather and temperature of a place.

**Detritivore:** a dinosaur or animal that only eats decomposing organic matter, like fungi and bacteria.

**Echinoderm:** an invertebrate, such as a starfish or a sea cucumber, that lives on the seabed and has spiny or bumpy skin.

**Habitat:** where a plant, animal, or dinosaur lives.

**Herbivore:** a dinosaur or animal that only eats plants.

**Invertebrate:** an animal with no spinal column.

**Omnivore:** a dinosaur or animal that eats both meat and plants.

**Paleontologist:** scientists who study fossils to learn more about prehistoric life.

**Predator:** a dinosaur or animal that hunts other dinosaurs or animals for food.

**Prehistoric:** things that existed before humans started writing things down.

**Prey:** a dinosaur or animal that is hunted by other dinosaurs or animals for food.

**Species:** a group of living things with the same characteristics.

**Terrain:** land or ground, and what's special about it (e.g., rocky or muddy).

**Tetrapod:** a land vertebrate with four legs.

**Vertebrate:** an animal with a spinal column.

# Contents

The Cambrian Period .................................................................. 6
The Ordovician Period ............................................................... 8
The Silurian Period ..................................................................... 9
The Devonian Period ................................................................ 10
The Carboniferous Period ........................................................ 12
The Permian Period .................................................................. 14
What is a Dinosaur? ................................................................. 16
Carnivore vs Herbivore ............................................................ 18
Dino Defenses ........................................................................... 20
Types of Dinosaurs ................................................................... 22
Life in the Oceans .................................................................... 24
Life in the Skies ......................................................................... 26
The Triassic Period ................................................................... 28
The Jurassic Period .................................................................. 30
The Cretaceous Swamps ......................................................... 32
The Cretaceous Plains ............................................................. 34
Extinction .................................................................................. 36
What Came Next? .................................................................... 38
The Neogene and Pleistocene Periods ................................... 40
Modern Dinosaurs .................................................................... 42
How Fossils Are Made .............................................................. 44
Mary Anning: Fossil Hunter .................................................... 45
Index .......................................................................................... 46

# The Cambrian Period

The Cambrian Period (542 million-485 million years ago) didn't have any land animals or plants. What it *did* have, however, were several creatures that lived in the oceans, including its most common animal, the trilobite...

### TRILOBITE
### OMNIVORE
Trilobites were arthropods. Some were predators (they hunted and ate other animals), while others may have simply eaten plankton. Some trilobites had a pair of eyes, but others had no eyes at all.

### ANOMALOCARIS
### CARNIVORE
Thought to be one of history's first apex predators.

### DID YOU KNOW?
Layered deposits known as stromatolites, made mostly of limestone, contained some of Earth's first forms of life. They came in a variety of shapes and still grow today—mostly in western Australia.

### KIMBERELLA
### OMNIVORE
Slug-like creatures called Kimberella are considered one of the first types of animal that could digest food through its gut. Other animals of this time are thought to have mainly absorbed food through their bodies.

At this time, there was a huge supercontinent called Gondwana. It was believed to have included modern-day Africa, India, Australia, Antarctica, Arabia, Madagascar, and South America.

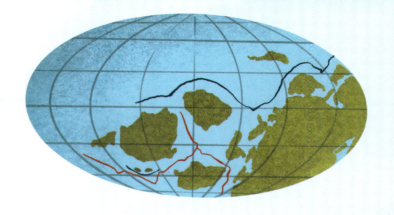

Volcanic activity along the seabed helped play a part in an event known as the "Cambrian explosion." Huge shifts in sea levels, flooding of continents, and an increase in oxygen within seawater all helped kick-start newer, more varied life on Earth.

**PIKAIA DETRITIVORE**

The seas included weird and wonderful creatures like Pikaia and Hallucigenia.

**HALLUCIGENIA DETRITIVORE**

# The Ordovician Period

The Ordovician Period (485 million-443 million years ago) was dominated by marine life. Sea levels were very high, with some continents almost entirely underwater.

By the end of the Ordovician Period, a large drop in sea levels and rapid cooling led to a mass extinction event...

Although they first appeared in the Cambrian Period, Trilobites were common throughout the Ordovician Period, too. Their bodies were divided into three parts: head, body, and tail.

**STARFISH CARNIVORE**
Still alive in today's oceans, starfish are not actually fish, but echinoderms. They usually have five arms which they use to move along the seabed.

**DID YOU KNOW?**
Some trilobites grew to almost 19 in. long—that's about the size of a bowling pin.

# The Silurian Period

The Silurian Period (443 million-419 million years ago) saw continents flooded with shallow seas. Gondwana covered large areas of the southern polar region. In the north, the planet was covered almost entirely by the ocean.

Coral mound reefs became more common, and these became the perfect place for jawed fish and other creatures to thrive.

Cephalopods (early forms of modern-day squid) were common throughout the Silurian seas. Species that could be found under the waves included ammonites, nautiloids, and belemnites.

**ACANTHODII
OMNIVORE**
Acanthodii are considered the earliest ever jawed fish. Also known as "spiny sharks," they had spines in front of their fins. These could have been used for defense, or to warn off larger predators.

Baragwanathia were some of the first plants with leaves, arranged up and along the stem. These ancient plants could grow up to 11 in. long.

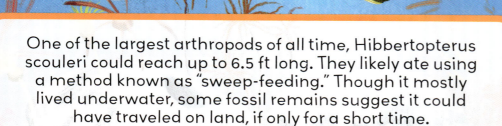

One of the largest arthropods of all time, Hibbertopterus scouleri could reach up to 6.5 ft long. They likely ate using a method known as "sweep-feeding." Though it mostly lived underwater, some fossil remains suggest it could have traveled on land, if only for a short time.

**BELEMNITE
CARNIVORE**

**HIBBERTOPTERUS SCOULERI
CARNIVORE**

# The Devonian Period

Sometimes called the "Age of Fishes," the Devonian Period (419 million-358 million years ago) featured lots of early marine and freshwater fish.

Gondwana still dominated the Southern Hemisphere. Further up toward the center, modern-day Europe and North America were joined together.

**DID YOU KNOW?**
Coelacanths are still around today, though they're about half the size of their ancestors!

**ACANTHOSTEGA
CARNIVORE**
Scientists think Acanthostega is one possible link between fish and the very first tetrapods capable of living on land. It's one of the first vertebrates with recognizable limbs.

**COELACANTH
CARNIVORE**
These huge fish could likely have been found all over the Devonian world. Some grew to around 6.5 ft in length, which is half as long as a small car.

**BOTHRIOLEPIS CANADENSIS
DETRIVORE**
This fish had small jaws and teeth. It would use its fins to "walk" along riverbeds, feeding on the invertebrates living there.

### ICHTHYOSTEGA
### CARNIVORE
These early amphibians were around 3 ft long. They're some of the earliest known vertebrates. They had scales along their body and bony supports in their tails.

### RHYNIOGNATHA HIRSTI
### OMNIVORE
This bug is considered the world's first-ever insect. Its fossil was first discovered in Scotland.

### DUNKLEOSTEUS
### CARNIVORE
An aggressive predator, Dunkleosteus had bony plates of armor all along its 20 ft long body. Due to the way its jaw opened and closed, the blades they used for cutting would be constantly sharpened by each other.

### TIKTAALIK
### CARNIVORE
Tiktaalik is one of the main creatures of this period that scientists have used to help them understand how some fish evolved to live on land.

### AMMONOID
### CARNIVORE
Ammonoids had distinctive shells which were used partly for protection, as well as to live in. They swam along in shallow waters hunting for food.

# The Carboniferous Period

358 million–298 million years ago, plants and animals were having to evolve to suit new environments, like swamp forests, that were created by tectonic plates moving. Since there were so many plants, it was known as the Carboniferous Period.

Unlike the trees of today, ferns from this period had trunks made from lots of tiny roots.

Horsetail plants are considered some of the oldest plants on the planet. They would have helped make up large parts of the many swamp forests of this period.

### DAIDAL SHRIMP
### CARNIVORE

Daidal shrimp are thought to have been predators because their forelegs might have been able to catch and hold prey. Some scientists believe it was a scavenger (meaning it ate animals already killed by something else).

### ARTHROPLEURA
### HERBIVORE

Arthropleura are the largest arthropods ever to have lived on Earth. They were as big as a car and would have eaten things like leaves, plants, nuts, and seeds.

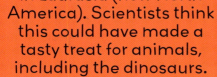

Cycad trees first appeared in Laurasia (now North America). Scientists think this could have made a tasty treat for animals, including the dinosaurs.

### SEA CUCUMBER
### OMNIVORE

Due to their soft bodies, sea cucumber fossils are rare, but some have been found in sedimentary rocks. This allowed paleontologists to discover all about the many and varied species that lived during prehistoric times.

### MEGANEURA
### CARNIVORE

Meganeura were similar to modern-day dragonflies (though much bigger at around 26 in. from wingtip to wingtip). They would swoop around Carboniferous habitats, chasing other insects to eat.

### MEGALOCEPHALUS
### CARNIVORE

Paleontologists have only ever found Megalocephalus' head, not its body! Its name means "big head"—and for good reason; it's 12 in. long. From this, paleontologists have been able to figure out that Megalocephalus was likely around 5 ft long in total.

### HYLONOMUS
### CARNIVORE

Hylonomus were small lizard-like animals that scurried around the new forest habitats during the Carboniferous Period.

### ACANTHODES
### CARNIVORE

Fossils have shown that shark-like Acanthodes were not only fast swimmers but also saw things in color—something not believed possible with other creatures of this time.

### PULMONOSCORPIUS
### CARNIVORE

Pulmonoscorpius was an early type of scorpion, though it was far larger than those you'd find around today. At an estimated length of 28 in. they were around the size of a cat from nose to tail.

# The Permian Period

The Permian Period (298 million-252 million years ago) began mostly covered in ice. The planet gradually warmed causing 90 percent of life on the planet to become extinct.

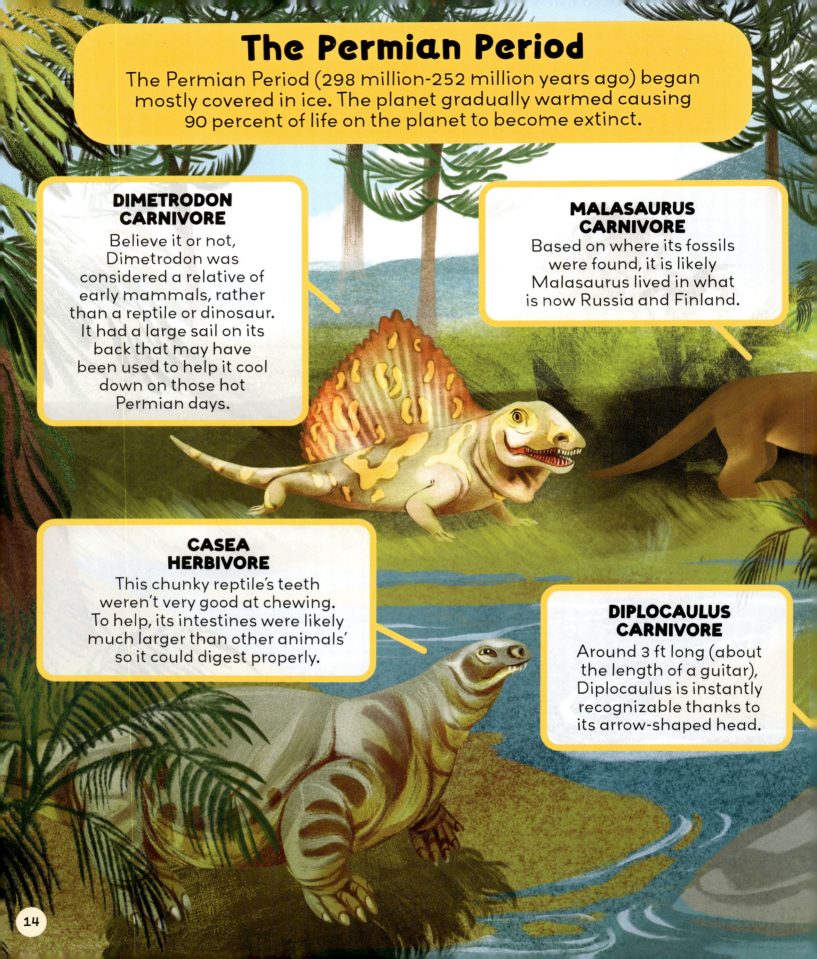

### DIMETRODON
### CARNIVORE

Believe it or not, Dimetrodon was considered a relative of early mammals, rather than a reptile or dinosaur. It had a large sail on its back that may have been used to help it cool down on those hot Permian days.

### MALASAURUS
### CARNIVORE

Based on where its fossils were found, it is likely Malasaurus lived in what is now Russia and Finland.

### CASEA
### HERBIVORE

This chunky reptile's teeth weren't very good at chewing. To help, its intestines were likely much larger than other animals' so it could digest properly.

### DIPLOCAULUS
### CARNIVORE

Around 3 ft long (about the length of a guitar), Diplocaulus is instantly recognizable thanks to its arrow-shaped head.

Shark-like Helicoprion had a unique jaw. Fossils show the teeth in its lower jaw arranged in a spiral. The largest of the teeth were around 4 in. long. Some scientists think this unique set of gnashers could have been used for de-shelling hard-bodied animals such as ammonoids.

### EDAPHOSAURUS
### HERBIVORE
Though it had a sail similar to Dimetrodons, Edaphosaurus was an herbivore and probably used its sail to appear more intimidating to any potential threats.

### DIADECTES
### HERBIVORE
Diadectes was one of the earliest land-living herbivores. It would use its front teeth to tear at plants and leaves, while its cheek teeth were used for chewing and grinding.

### ERYOPS
### CARNIVORE
Eryops was similar to a crocodile. It had eyes pointed upward at the top of its head, as well as a long jaw containing lots of sharp, pointy teeth.

# What is a Dinosaur?

Dinosaur means "terrible lizard." Dinosaurs first appeared during the Triassic Period before dominating the landscape in the Jurassic through to the end of the Cretaceous. They laid eggs like modern-day birds. Unlike reptiles, dinosaur legs were under their bodies. This meant they used less energy to move.

## QUETZALCOATLUS
### CARNIVORE

Though some dinosaurs could fly, the sky was mostly full of flying reptiles. Quetzalcoatlus, with a wingspan between 33-40 ft, was large enough to be a threat to smaller dinosaurs.

## VELOCIRAPTOR
### CARNIVORE

Not all dinosaurs were giants. The fearsome-looking predator Velociraptor, with its hook-shaped talons, was roughly the same height as a large turkey.

## PLESIOSAURUS
### CARNIVORE

Under the sea, huge beasts with sharp teeth swam the oceans. One of these creatures was Plesiosaurus. It is thought that this sea beast used its long neck to attack schools of fish. Its sharp teeth would then snatch them into its mouth for a tasty treat.

## DREADNOUGHTUS
### HERBIVORE

When people think of dinosaurs, they often think of them being huge. When it comes to Dreadnoughtus, they were absolutely right. This giant is believed to have been around 85 ft in length—that's as long as two fire trucks.

# Carnivore vs Herbivore

A carnivore is an animal that eats meat. This means they would prey on other dinosaurs for their food. Though some would attack other dinosaurs, others were more likely scavengers and would eat the remains of dead animals killed by other dinosaurs. An herbivore is a plant-eating dinosaur. They didn't eat other dinosaurs, but would feast on plants, moss, and tree leaves.

### T. REX
### CARNIVORE

T. rex was one of the most fearsome carnivores. Its teeth were around the same length as a pen. Though its arms were short, this didn't matter to T. rex, whose powerful jaws allowed it to clamp down on its prey and tear huge chunks of flesh away with each bite.

A meat-eating dinosaur's teeth were often sharp and jagged. This let it tear into prey more easily. They also helped it to grip its unlucky victim so it couldn't escape.

### COELOPHYSIS
### CARNIVORE

With a name meaning "hollow form," Triassic carnivore Coelophysis was a swift and agile hunter. Its big eyes were perfect for spotting small animals, while its long snout allowed it to burrow for tiny creatures living in the ground.

## EDMONTOSAURUS
### HERBIVORE

One of many types of hadrosaurs (also known as "duck-billed" dinosaurs), Edmontosaurus had over 1000 teeth for grinding its food.

## PSITTACOSAURUS
### HERBIVORE

Psittacosaurus, which means "parrot lizard," likely got its name due to its beak, which was similar to a parrot's. It could walk on either all four of its legs, or just two—which would have been very handy for reaching leaves on the branches of higher up trees.

A hadrosaur's teeth were flat. When chewing, this allowed it to grind down tough vegetation to make it easier to digest.

# Dino Defenses

Seeing a dinosaur such as T. rex or Allosaurus running toward you would have been a terrifying sight. However, herbivores had remarkable methods of protecting themselves. This would have given any attacker plenty to think about.

### ANKYLOSAURUS
### HERBIVORE

Heavily armored with thick, bony plates along the top of its body, Ankylosaurus was the tank of the prehistoric world. It could crush an attacker's bones by swinging the heavy, bony club on the end of its tail. Unless a predator was able to flip it over, it's likely any attack on this brute would see a carnivore go hungry for a little while longer.

### IGUANODON
### HERBIVORE

Some dinosaurs may have used their hands for defense against predators. Iguanodon, for example, had a large thumb spike on the end of each hand.

## STYRACOSAURUS
### HERBIVORE

Styracosaurus certainly lives up to its meaning ("spiked lizard") with those magnificent horns on its nose and frill. Those fearsome spikes could have been used as the perfect defense to keep carnivores a safe distance away.

## STEGOSAURUS
### HERBIVORE

Though its bony plates looked fearsome, they were mainly used to control body temperature and not for defense. Stegosaurus most likely used its tail to defend itself. The tail had four sharp spikes, called "thagomizers," on it.

# Types of Dinosaurs

Dinosaurs can be split into different groups, including the following:

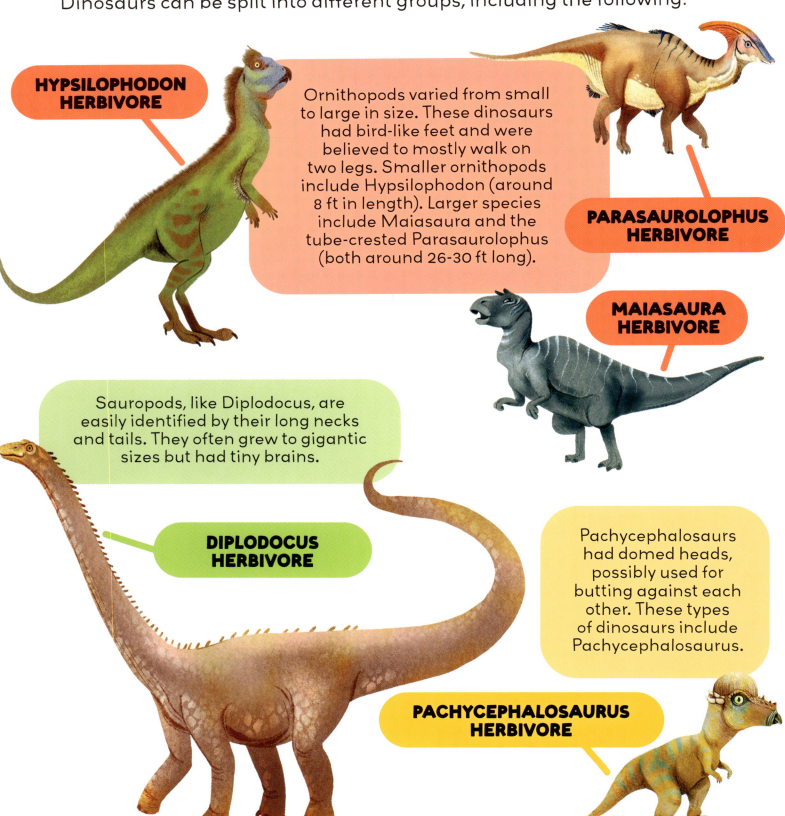

**HYPSILOPHODON HERBIVORE**

Ornithopods varied from small to large in size. These dinosaurs had bird-like feet and were believed to mostly walk on two legs. Smaller ornithopods include Hypsilophodon (around 8 ft in length). Larger species include Maiasaura and the tube-crested Parasaurolophus (both around 26-30 ft long).

**PARASAUROLOPHUS HERBIVORE**

**MAIASAURA HERBIVORE**

Sauropods, like Diplodocus, are easily identified by their long necks and tails. They often grew to gigantic sizes but had tiny brains.

**DIPLODOCUS HERBIVORE**

Pachycephalosaurs had domed heads, possibly used for butting against each other. These types of dinosaurs include Pachycephalosaurus.

**PACHYCEPHALOSAURUS HERBIVORE**

**CENTROSAURUS
HERBIVORE**

Ceratopsians had a wide variety of frills and facial horns. These four-legged herbivores included dinosaurs such as Centrosaurus.

**HUAYANGOSAURUS
HERBIVORE**

Stegosaurs are famous for the plates along their back and their spiky tails. Huayangosaurus is a stegosaur. It lived in the Jurassic period.

**SAUROPELTA
HERBIVORE**

Ankylosaurs were four-legged dinosaurs with armor-plated backs and a clubbed or spiky tail. Some ankylosaurs, like Sauropelta, had spikes to protect their necks.

Theropods include some of the most terrifying dinosaurs to ever walk the Earth, like Carnotaurus. Its arms were smaller than a T. rex's, and it had distinctive horns just above its eyes. Another theropod was Stenonychosaurus. For many years, experts thought fossils of this dinosaur actually belonged to Troodon. Stenonychosaurus is thought to have possibly been one of the smartest dinosaurs because its brain was quite large compared to the size of its body.

**CARNOTAURUS
CARNIVORE**

**STENONYCHOSAURUS
OMNIVORE**

# Life in the Oceans

From the Triassic through to the Cretaceous, the oceans were full of fascinating sea creatures.

### KRONOSAURUS
### CARNIVORE

If you were swimming in the seas of the early Cretaceous, there's a chance you would have met Kronosaurus, a 40 ft long pliosaur. Like all pliosaurs, Kronosaurus had a large head and short neck—its skull being roughly 12 ft long.

### ICHTHYOSAURUS
### CARNIVORE

Ichthyosaurus (meaning "fish lizard") had large eyes that helped it hunt fish in the dark depths of the Jurassic oceans. Fossils show that it gave birth to live young and didn't lay eggs like dinosaurs.

### WOOLUNGASAURUS
### CARNIVORE

Smaller plesiosaurs like Woolungasaurus would hunt even smaller reptiles such as turtles.

### CRETOXYRHINA
### CARNIVORE
Similar in look and size to a great white shark, what is known about Cretoxyrhina mostly comes from its fossilized teeth. These were up to 2 in. long and very sharp.

### ELASMOSAURUS
### CARNIVORE
At around 46 ft long, Elasmosaurus is one of the largest plesiosaurs ever discovered. Its long neck contained over 70 vertebrae —a human neck has only 7.

### PARAPLACODUS
### CARNIVORE
Alive during the Triassic period, Paraplacodus would most likely have been found in shallow waters searching for shellfish to eat.

# Life in the Skies

If you were walking with dinosaurs and looked up into the sky, you may have seen some of these stunning animals.

## TUPANDACTYLUS
### CARNIVORE

Tupandactylus is a pterosaur that would have stood out in the skies of the Cretaceous Period. It had a large, colorful crest on its head which scientists believe had short feathers around the base that could change color.

## YI QI
### CARNIVORE

Discovered in China in 2015, Yi Qi is different from other flying reptiles because its wing structure includes a soft tissue membrane that resembles those seen on bats.

## MICRORAPTOR
### CARNIVORE

Around the size of a pigeon, Microraptor, a theropod, had wings on both its arms and legs, and was covered in feathers. Unlike most flying reptiles, Microraptor was a dinosaur.

## QUETZALCOATLUS
### CARNIVORE

Quetzalcoatlus is one of the biggest flying animals of all time. It was the same size as a fighter jet. Powered by its huge wings, it could fly for thousands of miles without stopping.

## DARWINOPTERUS
## CARNIVORE

Scientists believe male Darwinopterus would have had larger crests on their heads than the females. They may have used these to warn off rivals.

## TROPEOGNATHUS
## CARNIVORE

Tropeognathus had a distinctive crest at the top and bottom end of its snout, though it was larger on top. Its wingspan was around 23-26 ft.

## PTERANODON
## CARNIVORE

With a long, toothless jaw like a pelican, Pteranodon lived during the late-Cretaceous and had a wingspan of around 23 ft.

## CAUPEDACTYLUS
## OMNIVORE

With a wingspan of just over 10 ft, Caupedactylus was thought to have been an omnivorous pterosaur, which meant it ate fish, meat, and plants.

# The Triassic Period

The Triassic Period (252 million-201 million years ago) was the first period in the Mesozoic Era (which included the Jurassic and Cretaceous). Animal life went through a big change in this period. Dinosaurs were starting to appear, but there were plenty of reptiles and mammals, too.

### EUDIMORPHODON
### CARNIVORE
Eudimorphodon was a pterosaur. Its jaw was only 2 in. long, but it had over 100 teeth.

### PLATEOSAURUS
### HERBIVORE
Plateosaurus had flat teeth that allowed it to crush and grind its food. Its five-fingered hands may have been used to rip plants from the ground or strip leaves off branches.

### POSTOSUCHUS
### CARNIVORE
At up to 23 ft long, Postosuchus was the largest land-based carnivore during the Triassic. It is thought to have been able to move around on both two and four legs like a bear.

### MORGANUCODON
### CARNIVORE
One of the earliest mammals discovered so far, tiny Morganucodon was only around 5 in. long.

### GUAIBASAURUS
### HERBIVORE
An ancestor of the later, larger sauropods, Guaibasaurus is only known from a few incomplete fossils.

# The Jurassic Period

The Jurassic Period (201 million-145 million years ago) was the second period in the Mesozoic Era. Dinosaurs started to dominate the landscape, though mammals lived during this period, too.

### RHAMPHORHYNCHUS
### CARNIVORE
This pterosaur had a tail with a diamond-shaped tip. This was likely used to help it change direction when flying. The way its teeth leaned forward made them perfect for catching and holding onto wiggly fish.

### SCELIDOSAURUS
### HERBIVORE
This dinosaur had ridged, bony scales embedded along its back and tail, similar to a crocodile.

### IGUANODON
### HERBIVORE
Iguanodon was able to walk on both two legs and all fours. To save energy, it would likely have only stood on two legs to make itself look more threatening to nearby predators.

### CASTOROCAUDA
### CARNIVORE
The largest known mammal in the Jurassic Period, Castorocauda was roughly the size of a platypus. It had a tail similar to a beaver's, which it likely used to help it swim while hunting for fish.

### STEGOSAURUS
### HERBIVORE
Stegosaurus (which means "roofed lizard") had large bony plates all along its back and tail. When it was first discovered, it was believed these plates lay flat on its back like a protective shell. This was proven to be wrong after more complete fossils were discovered.

### ALLOSAURUS
### CARNIVORE

Allosaurus was a massive meat-eater that was at the very top of the food chain. A fierce hunter, its mouth was packed with dozens of sharp, saw-edged teeth that helped it to rip and tear at flesh.

### APATOSAURUS
### HERBIVORE

Apatosaurus was a large sauropod thought to have lived in herds. It is believed to have taken an Apatosaurus about ten years to reach its full size—around 75 ft long!

### SCUTELLOSAURUS
### HERBIVORE

Scutellosaurus had bony lumps of armor which covered its back. Unlike more heavily armored dinos like Ankylosaurus, it was likely agile enough to run away from an attack if needed.

# The Cretaceous Swamps

The Cretaceous Period (145 million–66 million years ago) was cooler than previous eras. The continents as we know them today were taking shape and separating from each other. This created boggy habitats that many creatures thrived in...

**SPINOSAURUS
CARNIVORE**

Spinosaurus was one of the largest land-based carnivores around. Named for the huge sail on its back, it could grow up to 49 ft long and weigh as much as three elephants!

**EDMONTOSAURUS
HERBIVORE**

Edmontosaurus is thought to have spent much of its time in water.

**PSITTACOSAURUS
HERBIVORE**

Psittacosaurus was about the size of a large turkey. It had wide horns on its cheeks and used its beak to chomp away at leaves, nuts, and seeds.

# The Cretaceous Plains

Huge predators stalked this diverse terrain looking for food, while even larger sauropods ate leaves from the trees. The smaller herbivores ate plants closer to the ground.

### TRICERATOPS
### HERBIVORE

Triceratops had a bony frill around its head which likely protected its neck when under attack. To fight back, it had three horns on its head. The horns above each eye could sometimes be up to 3 ft long. That's the same size as a baseball bat.

### SALTASAURUS
### HERBIVORE

Saltasaurus was different from other sauropods since it is believed to have had small bony plates on its back. These would help protect it from predators large enough to take down a dinosaur of that size.

### PACHYCEPHALOSAURUS
### HERBIVORE

These two pachycephalosauruses are butting heads, most likely to see who is the strongest.

### DID YOU KNOW?

Of all the dinosaurs so far discovered, those living in the Cretaceous Period are more common than those from the Jurassic or Triassic.

### QUETZALCOATLUS
### CARNIVORE
Although it walked on two legs, the wings of Quetzalcoatlus were so large that it would have had to put its hands on the ground, too.

### T. REX
### CARNIVORE
T. rex was a fierce predator. It dominated the Cretaceous period, preying on other dinosaurs. Its strong jaws allowed it to crush bones with ease. With its massive skull, huge jaw muscles, and saw-edged teeth, T. rex had one of the strongest bites of any land animal ever.

### ORNITHOMIMUS
### OMNIVORE
A startled Ornithomimus flees from a hungry T. rex. Like an ostrich, its long legs helped it to run quickly.

## Extinction

Though dinosaurs were dominating the planet, there was nothing they could do when a meteor crashed into Earth around 66 million years ago. It caused a climate change catastrophe all around the world.

The aftermath of the impact resulted in 75 percent of all life on Earth becoming extinct. The age of the dinosaurs was over.

**DID YOU KNOW?**
The size of the crater made by the meteor when it hit the planet was around 12 miles deep.

# What Came Next?

The Paleogene Period was made up of the Paleocene Epoch (66 million-56 million years ago), Eocene Epoch (56 million-34 million years ago), and the Oligocene Epoch (34 million to 23 million years ago). Dinosaurs were now extinct, and this allowed other animals to spread across the planet, as well as marine life, too.

### PALAEOCHIROPTERYX
### CARNIVORE
Palaeochiropteryx was a small bat-like creature with a wingspan of between 10-12 in.

### PALAEEUDYPTES KLEKOWSKII
### CARNIVORE
Palaeeudyptes klekowskii is the largest penguin ever discovered at nearly 6.5 ft tall. Scientists believe that, thanks to its enormous size, it could stay underwater for around 40 minutes while it hunted for fish.

### TITANOBOA
### CARNIVORE
Titanoboa was a 43 ft long snake similar to boa constrictors and anacondas.

### UTAETUS
### CARNIVORE
Utaetus was an early type of armadillo.

### PLESIADAPIS
### HERBIVORE
Plesiadapis was one of the earliest primates ever discovered.

### RODHOCETUS
### CARNIVORE
Rodhocetus is believed to be an early type of whale and, because it had arms rather than flippers, it's possible that it could have walked on land.

# The Neogene and Pleistocene Periods

The Neogene Period is made up of the Miocene Epoch (23 million-5.3 million years ago) and the Pliocene Epoch (5.3 million-2.6 million years ago). This period led into the Pleistocene Period (2.6 million-11,700 years ago) which included the most recent ice age experienced on Earth.

**AEGYPTOPITHECUS HERBIVORE**

Creatures first around in the Miocene Epoch included: Gomphothere, a relative of modern-day elephants; Livyatan (a giant whale measuring nearly 60 ft long); Chalicotherium (an ancient rhinoceros); and Aegyptopithecus (related to modern day apes and primates).

**GOMPHOTHERE HERBIVORE**

The Pliocene Epoch also featured many amazing creatures such as Dromornis, a large flightless bird (around 8 ft tall) similar to an ostrich. In prehistoric Australia, a carnivorous marsupial known as Thylacoleo wandered the landscape.

**CHALICOTHERIUM HERBIVORE**

**THYLACOLEO CARNIVORE**

**LIVYATAN CARNIVORE**

Megatherium was a giant ground sloth. Around the same size as an elephant, Megatherium dug large stone tunnels underground called paleoburrows. Most of these are being discovered in South America.

The oldest fossil skeleton of an ancestor to humans came from the Pliocene Epoch. These human relatives were called Australopithecus, and the particular fossil discovered in 1974 was nicknamed "Lucy."

**WOOLLY MAMMOTH HERBIVORE**

With its thick, hairy coat, the woolly mammoth was perfectly suited to surviving cold temperatures. Early humans painted this elephant-sized animal on cave walls.

**DROMORNIS OMNIVORE**

**AUSTRALOPITHECUS OMNIVORE**

**SMILODON CARNIVORE**

Smilodon was a cat-like carnivore with canine teeth that grew up to 8 in. long.

Descending from ape-like creatures, humans as we know them today are called homo sapiens. There were different species that were part of the development of man ("homo") called Australopithecus afarensis, Homo habilis, Homo erectus, and Homo neanderthalensis. Humans are believed to have been around for about 300,000 years.

# Modern Dinosaurs

All around the planet are animals which have evolved over millions of years. Most have links to animals that lived in prehistoric times.

**T. REX CARNIVORE**

**HOATZIN HERBIVORE**
With its young having two large claws on each wing, some scientists have wondered if this crested bird has links to the flying dinosaur, Archaeopteryx.

**TUATARA CARNIVORE**
Once found throughout the planet millions of years ago, tuataras are now only found in New Zealand. They also have a hidden third eye on the top of their head!

Scientists believe chickens are descendants of T. rex, one of the greatest, most powerful predators to have walked the earth.

**CHICKEN HERBIVORE**

**CROCODILE CARNIVORE**
These apex predators have barely evolved from how they were millions of years ago. Though smaller in many cases, they still look the same as prehistoric crocodiles such as Sarcosuchus.

## PARAILURUS
### HERBIVORE

Parailurus was around 50 percent bigger than today's red pandas. Fossils show it lived in Europe, Asia, and North America in the Pliocene Epoch.

## RED PANDA
### HERBIVORE

Red Pandas aren't bears but are instead closely related to raccoons. The name "panda" means "bamboo-eater."

## OSTRICH
### OMNIVORE

This flightless bird's ancestors date back to the Eocene Epoch. It can run as quickly as 43.5 miles per hour when escaping predators.

## HORSESHOE CRAB
### OMNIVORE

Horseshoe crabs have been around for over 300 million years. They are not actually crabs, but are more closely related to extinct trilobites.

## GOBLIN SHARK
### CARNIVORE

Mostly found in deep waters near Japan, the goblin shark has a long forehead spike. It's likely used to help it "see" in the murky depths of the ocean.

# How Fossils Are Made

After a dinosaur dies, its body decomposes, leaving a skeleton.

Over time, the skeleton sinks into a layer of mud, where it becomes buried.

Layers of mud, sand, ash, and lava build up on top of the skeleton, squishing it down.

Over time, the earth moves upward and the rock is slowly worn away.

The fossil is exposed by wind and rain, ready to be found by paleontologists (dino experts).

Once the fossil has been studied, it is displayed in a museum for everyone to see!

# Mary Anning: Fossil Hunter

Mary Anning (1799–1847) was an English fossil hunter. Her amazing discoveries helped scientists understand prehistoric life and extinction (when a whole species dies out). Mary discovered that bullet-shaped **belemnites** had fossilized ink sacs, like squid. She would also sell the ammonite fossils she found to collectors.

**BELEMNITE**

**AMMONITE**

One of Mary Anning's most famous finds was an **Ichthyosaur** skeleton. Scientists first thought it might be a crocodile or even a relative of the platypus, but eventually realized they were looking at the bones of an ancient sea creature.

# Index

**A**
Acanthodes..................13
Acanthodii....................9
Acanthostega..............10
Aegyptopithecus..........40
Allosaurus...................31
ammonites................9, 45
ammonoids..................11
ankylosaurs.................23
Ankylosaurus..............20
Anning, Mary..............45
Anomalocaris................6
Apatosaurus................31
Arizonasaurus.............29
armadillos...................38
Arthropleura................12
Australopithecus..........41

**B**
Baragwanathia..............9
bats.............................38
belemnites................9, 45
birds......................42, 43
Bothriolepis canadensis...10

**C**
cactuses......................39
Caelestiventus..............29
Cambrian Period........6–7
camels........................39
Carboniferous Period...12–13
carnivores...............18–19
Carnotaurus................23
Casea.........................14
Castorocauda..............30
Caupedactylus............27
Centrosaurus..............23
cephalopods..................9
ceratopsians...............23
Chalicotherium...........40

chickens......................42
coelacanths.................10
Coelophysis.................18
Compsognathus...........35
Cretaceous Period...16, 32–33, 34–35
Cretoxyrhina...............25
crocodiles....................42
cycads........................12

**D**
Daidal shrimp..............12
Darwinopterus.............27
defences..................20–21
Devonian Period......10–11
Diadectes....................15
Dimetrodon.................14
Diplocaulus.................14
Diplodocus..................22
Dreadnoughtus............17
Dromornis...................41
Dunkleosteus...............11

**E**
echinoderms..................8
Edaphosaurus..............15
Edmontosaurus........19, 32
Elasmosaurus..............25
elephants....................40
Entelodonts.................39
Eocene Epoch..............38
Eryops........................15
Eudimorphon...............28
extinction..........8, 14, 36–37

**F**
ferns.......................12, 39
fishes..........................10
flying reptiles...........26–27
fossils.....................44–45

**G**
goblin sharks...............43
Gomphothere..............40
Gondwana............7, 9, 10
Guaibasaurus..............28

**H**
hadrosaurs..................19
Hadrosaurus................33
Hallucigenia..................7
Helicoprion..................15
herbivores...........18–19, 20
Hibbertopterus scouleri...9
hoatzins......................42
Homo species..............41
horses..........................9
horseshoe crabs...........43
horsetails....................12
Huayangosaurus.........23
humans.......................41
Hylonomus..................13
Hypsilophodon............22

**I**
Ichthyosaurus..........24, 45
Ichthyostega................11
Iguanodon..............20, 30
Indricotherium............39

**J**
Jurassic Period........30–31

**K**
Kimberella....................6
Kronosaurus................24

**L**
Livyatan.....................40
llamas........................39